INTO TH

Forensic Interview with John Orr
"The Most Prolific Serial Arsonist
of the 20th Century"

Anthony Meoli

Other Books and Audio by Anthony Meoli

Books:

Diary of the D.C. Sniper

Audio (CD or MP3 Downloads):

"Interview with the D.C. Sniper" – Interview with Lee Boyd Malvo (2014)

"I Kill for God" – Interview with Washington State spree shooter Isaac Zamora (2014)

"The Kenneth Bianchi Interview – The Real Facts of Overview into the Bellingham, Washington and Hillside Strangler Murders" (2016)

About the Author

Education

John Marshall Law School – Doctor of Jurisprudence

Argosy University – M.A., Clinical Mental Health Counseling

Argosy University – M.A., Forensic Psychology

The Pennsylvania State University – B.S., Administration of Justice

Nationally Certified Counselor

Academic and Professional Associations:
APA, ACA, AISOCC, ACFEI and the NBCC

Inmate Contact Methodology

I have been writing and speaking to inmates for over two decades. My communication includes handwritten correspondence, telephonic communication, e-mails, video visitation and sometimes personal visitation.

I have personally visited nearly a dozen serial killers. Some of the inmates with whom I have spoken with or personally visited include Charles Manson, Elmer Wayne Henley, Phillip Carl Jablonski, Richard Ramirez, Danny Rolling, Glen Rogers, Lee Boyd Malvo,

Stanley Fitzpatrick, Isaac Zamora, Kenneth Bianchi, Karen Eckman, Loran Cole, Ramon Salcido, Michael Madison and John Orr.

The FBI's Behavioral Analysis Unit was well-known for visiting and sitting inside the cells of noted serial killers to gather information. It is my opinion that personal contact is essential to getting the inmate's version of events on record. Without such contact, it is merely speculation.

Six Minutes, a blog about public speaking, analyzed nine "Ted Talks" and found, "the average spoken word count was around 163 words per minute" (Dugan, 2017). Since the average letter from an inmate is typically 2-3 pages in length, a single conversation is analogous to writing and receiving letters for almost three months.

Additionally, speaking with an inmate makes the personal connection abundantly deeper, their cases become clearer, and the information gained is exponentially higher. I believe that unlike traditional writers who never actually speak with the inmate directly (with whom they are writing about), this method provides the information to be disseminated in a more succinct manner.

In the case of several inmates, my conversations with them have exceeded a decade. I do not consider regularly speaking to serial killers and murderers as "friendship," but rather look at it as simple human contact. We all need human contact, even those who have committed terrible things. When you offer an inmate with an unbiased listening ear, much can be gained for both parties.

Regardless of guilt or innocence, detailed case information is rarely divulged by inmates for numerous reasons. Sometimes an inmate does not want to risk their ongoing appellate issues. At other times it is because inmates are well aware the prison is recording their calls and perusing their outgoing mail. Therefore, any admission(s) therein could draw legal repercussions. It may also be for a rather simple reason - they do not want to talk about their case.

Contrary to popularly held beliefs, not all serial killers, murderers or prisoners enjoy speaking about what they did. On many occasions I have had an inmate break down over the phone while speaking about their actions. Most authors do not delve this deeply into the convicted criminal's mind which is what separates this style of information gathering.

Over the years there have been questions regarding inmate "self-reporting." The idea is that they have a reason to lie or will malinger within their answers to sway public opinion or get additional press. This is surely a possibility, but it does not, in any way, negate their interview. The point is to get the inmate on the record from their perspective. Whether they are lying or telling the truth, it is within their answers. It is up to the reader to decide and decipher what they believe given all of the information provided.

While this book is not lengthy by the average book's standards, this is largely due mistaken information being removed. This book cuts directly into Orr's life, relationships, work experiences and the events leading up to his arrest. The information is fully authorized and was obtained directly from John Orr.

Introduction

John Orr is believed to have set over 2,000 fires from 1984-1991. Four innocent people were murdered during one of these blazes. These acts were committed by a sworn officer hired and trained to protect the public from the very person he came to be - a serial arsonist. These are the accusations and murder convictions of John Leonard Orr, who has been named "The Most Prolific Arsonist of the 20th Century."

The relationship between John Orr and myself is an interesting one. We both have respect for one another, regardless of the crimes that were alleged to have occurred. Respect is a tough concept for some to understand but without it, rarely do successful communications occur. I do not view John as a "monster" to be torn down further. I have chosen to delve as deeply as he would let me, so that I could better understand who he is through this forensic interview. This interview reveals Orr's familial life, provides a better understanding of his relationships with four former wives, children, friends and co-workers. Finally, it examines whether this individual could commit the acts for which he now serves a sentence of life without the possibility of parole (LWOP).

Our relationship began as it did with all the inmates whom I have corresponded over the years, with just a simple letter. The letter was two pages long and consisted of who I was and why I was interested in getting to know him. All the while, divulging details that could be researched by him to vet me out.

If an inmate does not think you are who you say you are, or that your promises will fall flat, they will not respond. It is just that simple. Trust is the bedrock of any relationship. If there is no trust, the relationship will not last and no information will never be gained.

The pen pal relationship between myself and any inmate often hinges on a paragraph, sentence or even a single word. One word, used or interpreted the wrong way, can send the relationship downhill. As quickly as it begins, the relationship can end even faster. It is their perception of how you come across which matters, not yours. To that end, I treat every inmate with the utmost of respect. Vilifying them further gets me nowhere.

Our written communication went from sparse missives to writing fairly regularly within a very short time, which was unexpected. In my experience with inmates, it is typical to receive one to two letters per month, depending on the location of the inmate, the health of the inmate, and the sincerity of keeping the relationship fresh. This can also change by the days of the week mail goes out along with the overall amount of mail that particular inmate receives. Some inmates might receive up to 200 letters per day (Charles Manson) while other inmates might receive less than 200 letters per year.

Inmates receive all kinds of letters. Letters range from men acting as women to get a response, women acting as if they are their "destined soulmate," police needing information about cold cases and the list goes on. Whenever an inmate opens a letter they have many choices. In some cases, inmates will simply choose to throw out the letter or refuse the mail entirely. When an inmate refuses mail, it comes back to marked as such – "refused by inmate." In the case of a refusal to correspond, the envelope might still be sealed (as is often the case) or resealed and then sent back to the sender.

My first communication received from John Orr was in early 2017. Our letters increased in frequency to the point where I was receiving his letters two to three times per week. By the second month of writing, John and I had exchanged over two dozen letters. Each letter was averaging over seven pages. By May 2017, Orr had agreed to have this interview published along with an audio interview. He included dozens of never-before-seen original photos, newspaper articles and other evidentiary issues that he felt compelled to share. In each case, his items were copied with his full permission, then sent back.

As my letters grew longer, his own responses mirrored mine – increasing in page length with each writing. I realized that Orr would be more responsive to someone who actually read his books ("Points of Origin" and "Points of Truth"), understood his case and could see both sides of the story - while challenging him in the process.

When I first proposed the idea for a written interview, he was somewhat reluctant. John had been interviewed a few times previously, but never in detailed print. I explained that I had read his first book, "Points of Origin" (which depicts a fictitious arsonist who is also a firefighter), and most of his second book "Points of Truth" (which depicts John explaining how his conviction was erroneous based upon numerous factors including evidentiary issues and ineffective assistance of counsel). I had read both with an open mind.

The first book was clearly a work of fiction, and the second did contain actual information that was indeed true – there were some discrepancies about how his case had been portrayed. However, there is a difference between keeping one's mind open and being directed to do something.

I assured John that my interview would include the facts, but delve into getting to know him. He would be challenged on some of the evidentiary issues. At a bare minimum, I would try to present the interview chronologically so readers could quickly learn his case.

What struck a chord with John was that I had degrees in both law and psychology. He knew that I could comprehend the concepts he was putting forth and understood my need to know the truth of how an individual could commit such acts – if indeed he had perpetuated them.

As our letters increased, my request to have him contact me by phone was met with little resistance. The reason for the phone calls was to provide another way to communicate with him and to humanize both of us. Letters are very stale. They do not provide much in the way of intimacy and neither party feels what the other wants to say or how they really meant to say it. One phone call erases that completely.

The importance of speaking directly with the inmate can be many-fold. A phone call or personal visit allows for subjective interpretation. Observations that can be made include tonal inflection, affect, mood, health (coughing, prison conditions, etc.), and subtle nuances that may indicate possible malingering. The calls provide more humanistic behavior towards one another. This type of communication also allows for the ability to correct, amend or even apologize for any previous letters that may have offended the inmate, offended you or to simply drill down on the specifics of any letter needing further clarification.

I have fielded calls from serial killers and murderers for as long as I can remember. It is not uncommon for me to receive five calls a week from those who have committed serial acts of violence.

Inmates do not always get phone time and between my obligations of family, jobs and all of the other things that consume most people's lives, many phone calls are never received. Over the years I have missed far more calls than I have received. I have also ruined many family dinners when taking these calls. Even when the inmate has set a day and time, and provided assurances they will call, things come up on their end. Some of those things could include "lock down," inmate health issues, meeting with lawyers or being reprimanded (no phone calls allowed). Other times, the phone might ring and when I accept their call – the call simply hangs up. You often get one shot at an inmate phone call. If the inmate has a dozen people behind him and that call does not go through, you do not get a chance to talk.

In John Orr's case, I did not know when or if he was ever going to call. As he explained in one of his letters from Centinela State Prison, "I do not know when I can get phone time, but hopefully you will be home." Eventually, we connected. We worked out a schedule that led to a half-dozen calls (20 minutes per call) that helped clarify the information you are about to read.

I did request that any addendums or additional information about a particular question be sent in writing. This was to ensure that I could transcribe his answers verbatim to his own text. John complied and those additions were incorporated into the interview.

By no means can one book capture all the nuances of John Orr's case. It is my expectation that you will learn more about his case along with the evidentiary and legal issues presented that both convicted him or needed further interpretation. It is my belief that enough information is covered for those wanting to get the information directly from "the most prolific serial arsonist of the 20th century."

Anthony Meoli

What is Arson?

Arson is defined as, "the criminal setting of fires, deliberate burning or property by fire, fire raising, firing, malicious burning or property and willful burning or charring of property on purpose." (Burton, 2007) The act of arson may also include setting fire to property to collect insurance money, commit a crime or even to cover a previous criminal act. Arson may also include the burning of cars, boats, personal property and land. In rare cases, fire is set merely for the gratification of the "fire setter."

Serial Arsonist Statistics

Lewis and Yarnell (1951) found that the vast majority of fire setters are males with only 14.8% of serial arsonists being female. Although the 1951 study is somewhat dated, a study three decades later agreed that females accounted for approximately 10%-18% of arsonists. (Bradford, 1982) Current estimates indicate that females account for 10-12% of all serial arsonists. Arson fires, which are those that contain either an incendiary device or are listed as "suspicious," comprised nearly 16% of all reported fires in 1997. These acts of arson accounted for more than $554 million in losses. (FEMA, 1997)

What often goes unnoticed with serial arsonists is the incredible amount of destruction left behind. Arsonists cause huge financial losses to individuals and businesses along with lasting emotional and physical scarring that never fully heals.

Profiling the Serial Arsonist

Serial arsonists are typically individuals whose repeated actions become a compulsion. These compulsive acts lead to serial acts of three or more separate fire setting episodes. The definition of the serial arsonist is comparable to that of a serial killer where 2 or more individuals are killed, with a "cooling off period" between the violent acts. As with serial killers, the serial arsonist may go dormant for a period of time, only to resurface weeks, months or even decades later.

Serial arsonists like to incite fear while watching their actions take place. They are voyeuristic by nature. Many arsonists revel in the act of not only watching the fire grow, but seeing the destruction their fires create. It is not uncommon for fire setters to have some experience with law enforcement or even be involved with putting fires out. It is this experience that allows them to create devices that will cause damage quickly.

The serial arsonist is often male. When a serial arsonist begins, he is often younger those who commit a single act of arson. On average, serial arsonists will have less than average education and often have difficulty in social situations. These traits can explain why many serial arsonists experience difficulty when trying to cultivate long-lasting relationships.

Research suggests that serial arsonists often live close to where they set their fires, generally not straying more than a few miles from scene of the crime. (Douglas & Burgess, 1992) In most cases, the arsonist has visited the location long before the fire was set or fantasized about that particular location.

In John Orr's case, he had often been called an "early arrival" fire inspector. This meant he was at the scene shortly after the fires began and often mystified other fire inspectors with his ability to predict and solve cases.

The serial arsonist, especially one who is familiar with crime scenes or works as a fire investigator, can explain their presence at the point of origin/crime scene. If the serial arsonist is involved with law enforcement, the arsonist is likely to inject himself into the investigation. The serial arsonist becomes experienced after some time and will often develop their own incendiary device. This becomes their "signature" in many ways. The device is usually crafted in such a way as to avoid detection or incinerate within the fire.

Preface by John Orr

I received your interview questionnaire today and will try to complete it to the best of my abilities. I was unable to schedule a phone call this time to clarify some of the questions, but I will instead, explain some of my concerns before answering.

Your references (statistical references) and chronology are understood but there are a few "foul balls" in the mix – the questions (some of them) are in error when relating to the retail warehouse fires in Glendale, California and my involvement in the investigation. The investigations I am referring to include the "Pillow Pyro" and "Frito Bandito" (snack foods and grocery fires) cases. I will explain these in my responses herein.

First off, there are no true "warehouse fires." The retail fires were home improvement outlets (Ole's, Lowes, Home Depot, etc.), department stores, fabric stores, etc. All were open for business with customers present, as opposed to a "warehouse" with just employees around. You also persist that as an investigator, I was directly involved in several "series fires" that were scattered around the state - I was not. However, the exception being, I was contacted by actual active case investigators seeking clues from other agencies, mine included. Since there is so little space provided on some of your questions, I will have to refer you to my addendums to provide complete answers.

In most of my case investigations, I relied on what the scene was telling me in the "who-done-it" cases. Those with the suspect known and/or those with the suspect named, I put them on the backburner while I processed scene profiling, then researched the suspect's background and his relationship to the victim and victim's history. Past history, actions and criminal background are not presentable in court, (or so I thought back in the day) so I focused on my gut feelings and they were usually correct.

I was so busy trying to defend myself during the completion of your questionnaire than I did on your more critical needs for further information. Context is difficult in our arrangement since I lean more towards your legal background and in trying to prove my innocence when it is your psychology background that is actually conducting this interview.

As to your legal background, I understand your concerns. To add more, again, the "uncharged acts" evidence was a large portion of the two federal cases, evidentiary hearings and the arson/murder trial and sentencing.

In the murder trial, there were a total of seven counts (with one count involving a brushfire that extended to eighteen (18) properties, resulting in the twenty-five (25) counts). None of the seven (7) counts could stand alone without the "uncharged acts" evidence. No (incendiary) devices were found, at least two to three which were probably accidental fires, and the linchpin was that the prosecution was allowed to reveal my coerced guilty plea in a federal case of "similar fires" in their opening statements.

As soon as the jury heard the prosecution's opening statements there was no need for a trial. I could have been convicted before the first witness was heard. My own lawyers stated/confirmed in their opening statement that, "Yes, Mr. Orr admitted to doing bad things

and he is a bad person for that…but he is innocent of these charges…"
No defendant can vindicate himself after an attack like that from both
sides – without testifying himself. I intended to testify but my lawyers
never prepared me and in the middle of the first day of the defense side
of the trial presentation, I overheard my two lawyers discussing
finishing up the next day!

They refused to allow me to answer questions and speculations
offered to the jury by the prosecution. I see you read "Points of Truth"
(John Orr's second book that details inconsistencies of his conviction
and improper representation by his defense counsel), in its entirety,
especially the last five chapters concerning the murder trial and my
lawyer's failings that amounted to ineffective counsel. Not included in
my book is the statement made by my second chair, (Mr. Rucker),
about his relationship with Mr. Giannini, (lead defense counsel), to my
legal assistant, (girl-friend) Christine Blanchett, post-trial. In a candid
moment, Rucker said he was thoroughly disappointed with how the
trial went and Giannini's tactics and strategies. Rucker was pleased he
was instrumental in getting me out from under the death penalty threat,
but soured on the division of responsibilities during preparation and in
trial.

Rucker had solely worked on the Ole's arson/murder and
Giannini handled other charges and all the "uncharged acts" defense.
Unfortunately, that division did not allow Rucker to examine the two
bracketing market fires that took place on the same evening as the
Ole's arson/murder. They also did not present how my alibi witness

placed me successfully out of the ignition sequence of the second market fire and Ole's.

My appointed direct appeal lawyer refused to entertain an ineffective counsel tactic, instead focusing on the "uncharged acts" issues and telling the jury in the opening statement that I confessed (guilty plea bargain), which were admittedly stronger issues. My court appointed lawyer, also said I should preserve the ineffective counsel issue for a future appeal. This is important to note for the simple fact since you cannot bring it up in subsequent appeals (which is good advice since newly discovered evidence is where I now hang my hat on for a future appeal).

Rucker apparently showed reluctance to repeat what he said to Ms. Blanchett about Giannini's ineffectiveness. As I recall, Rucker told Ms. Blanchett, "It is too soon after John's conviction for me to speak out regarding Giannini still owing me fees from John's trial." Rucker might support ineffective counsel claims now, but I do not know.

The Interview of John Orr

Anthony Meoli: For those who are unfamiliar with your name and case, could you please provide your full name and the exact sentence for which you were convicted:

John Orr: John Leonard Orr.

Federal Case: Serving 30 years (only one-third of the time required to satisfy the sentence); I paroled after 10 years to state custody. My Federal 30-year sentence expires in July 2022. State Case: Life without parole. My conviction includes four (4) counts of murder. I was found guilty of more than two dozen fires which included the October 10, 1984 blaze that took the lives of four people including: 17-year-old Jimmy Cetina, 26-year-old Carolyn Kraus, 50-year-old Ada Deal and her 2-year-old grandson, Matthew Troidl.

Meoli: When were you born and where did you grow up as a child?

Orr: I was born on April 26, 1949, (68 years old now), in Glendale, California. I grew up in nearby Highland Park/Eagle Rock areas of Northeast Los Angeles, California.

Meoli: Without specifically naming them, how many siblings do you have and where do you fall (birth order) among them?

Orr: Oldest brother (1945), middle brother (1946) and me (1949).

Meoli: Who do you recall as being the primary care-giver while you were growing up?

Orr: My mother almost always worked (after we were pre-teens) and both Dad and Mom provided pre-school prep, as well as after-school follow-up. Dad prepared dinner more often than Mom as well as helping us with homework, monitoring chores, etc. A very efficient team that seemed to come naturally from grandparents, who also shared home responsibilities.

Meoli: What do you remember as your fondest childhood memory?

Orr: Feeling safe and secure in our home with outstanding vacations to Arizona, Utah, Colorado and California. We all loved to travel and explore (many times with an aunt/uncle).

Meoli: If you are comfortable with sharing, what was your most upsetting childhood memory?

Orr: Probably coming home from a week-long vacation to find our water heater had ruptured and flooded our entire home – floors buckled (hardwoods), carpets drenched, furniture destroyed, etc. The Mom/Dad team provided reassurance that everything would be fine. Dad took another week off and we kids were included in salvage/repairs, a typical family operation.

Meoli: What is the highest level of education you obtained and where did you go to school?

Orr: I graduated from high school in 1967 (Eagle Rock High School, L.A. School District). I accumulated over 60 units in Junior College – mostly job/career related; I did not want to waste time taking standard courses (Math, Bio/Science, etc.) to achieve an Associates of Arts degree or higher. Some units granted were only for one day to one week long in-service training.

Meoli: The profile suggested the arsonist would have had difficulties with relationships. You were married four times. Can you explain what went wrong in these relationships?

Orr: 1st-Married too young (age 18), first year in military. After my discharge, I selfishly tried to capture my perceived "missed opportunities post high school" and initiated divorce instead of maturely trying to work on the problems.

2nd-Married spontaneously (Las Vegas) after one year of dating/living together. Not compatible.

3rd-Right woman with three beautiful daughters and potential to establish a nurturing family and excellent compatibility but "power" issues interfered. I worked a lot early on in my fire investigator career. I wanted support so I could advance; she also wanted a career, instead of our agreed-upon, white-picket fence lifestyle pre-marriage.

4th-Effects of my life without parole (LWOP) sentence ended the relationship – mutual agreement.

Meoli: As a Fire/Arson Investigator, would you have agreed with the criminal profile in that the arsonist would have had difficulties with relationships?

Orr: I agree with this aspect of the general arsonist profile of such an offender having difficulty with relationships. In my experience of apprehending, *"series fire" setters as juveniles/adults, the adults seemed uneasy with people in general and had few (or no) close friends. They tended to act inappropriately in groups as well as dealing with day to day interactions such as job interface, dealing with neighbors and on-the-street encounters. It seemed basic insecurity was at the root of their unease.

*Those setting over 40 fires.

Meoli: It has been written that you had failed a police entry examination and that is why you became a fireman. Is this correct information?

Orr: Upon release from the military, I sought a firefighter career and took four entrance exams, passing all and placed on lists that expired after two years. Thousands of applicants (post Viet Nam), lined up for these jobs. Getting to test was a huge success, but getting on the waitlist did not guarantee a job within the two-year life of the list, thus, it could be three to four years, or more, before being hired as a fireman. So, I took two police department exams, passing the Los Angeles Police Department (LAPD) written, physical and oral (so this cancelled the Los Angeles Sheriff's exam procedure). The psychological test showed I had some passivity and probably immaturity. (I was 23 at the time and still reeling from a pending divorce with two infants), so the LAPD passed on me with a recommendation to re-test after several years.

Meoli: At what point in your life did you decide that fire investigation interested you?

Orr: After four years of basic fire-fighting experience, I was assigned to the Fire Patrol Unit where I was taxed with enforcing fire prevention codes and hazardous materials laws. I liked it and was very good at it.

Meoli: Where did you obtain your fire investigation training and what did it involve?

Orr: When I first became interested in fire law enforcement, I found I needed more than on-the-job training and learn-as-you-go education. Offenders wanted to resist, avoid and evade by violence and I had no training. I got the basics of law enforcement through ride-alongs with uniformed officers (sanctions by both fire and police staff) and college courses in administration of Justice/Police Science. Fire and arson investigation was part of the job as patrolmen, so I took one Fire Technology course at the junior college level and a similar Fire Cause/Origin course through UCLA. This led to attendance at training seminars at the local and state levels. Exceptional arrest and investigation results early on, led me to join the state Arson Investigators Organization (California Conference of Arson Investigators, CCAI). The CCAI offered a state-certified course of four, one week long sessions that led to a Level I, then Level II investigator status. I completed the four-week course in 1980, just one week before appointment as Glendale's first full-time Arson Investigator. I later (1985) became one of only five individuals in California certified to teach the final week-long class and administer the final examination.

Meoli: What were your actual titles when you worked for the City of Glendale, California?

Orr: From 1974-1977: Firefighter.
From 1977-1980: Fire Patrolman/Firefighter.
From 1980-1986: Fire/Arson Investigator.
From 1986-1989: Senior Investigator.
From 1989-1992: Fire Captain.

Meoli: How long did you work as an Arson/Explosives Investigator?

Orr: Fourteen years.

Meoli: When did you first realize you and your department were dealing with a serial arsonist?

Orr: No context here. You seem under the impression the retail fires (nicknamed the "Pillow Pyro") affected Glendale – they did not. We had one "chip" fire, (nicknamed the "Frito Bandito"), on our border with Burbank, California in which the "Orr Device," which consisted of a cigarette, matches and rubber bands was recovered. I have an alibi for that fire. My partner, Dennis Wilson, and I were at a bar, together, at the time. This and another "potato chip" fire also occurred. Prosecutors did speculate I was involved with these fires.

Meoli: As the fires began to accumulate in number, were they strictly limited to areas where you lived, worked or attended annual fire conferences?

Orr: Original series of retail fires noted, were in Los Angeles/Orange County in the early 1980's, ("chip" fires relate back to the 1970's). Then came the Fresno area series. We were not aware of other retail series fires, but they may have occurred. The Central Coast series, two years after the Fresno fires occurred, which included the Saline area fires (4 fires) with a suspect. The Los Angeles' fires started around 1990-1991. In these series, 3 fires over a 10-year period, I lived, worked or traveled near all except the Orange County areas. Not all 3 series fires seemed directly related.

Meoli: When did you first realize, and try to be as specific if you can, that you were being investigated for the very crimes you were an expert at detecting?

Orr: I became aware that I was a suspect on December 4, 1991, at the moment of arrest. I wrote the chapter in *"Points of Origin", a fictional manuscript, about the protagonist being a suspect and surveilled in Fresno eight (8) months before I became a suspect. This chapter was actually penned months before the actual surveillance. When I discovered a tracking device on my car in May 1991, I had no idea why it was there and was reassured by authorities in which I contacted, the tracker was a joke perpetuated by training staff.

*A manuscript investigators believed only the arsonist could have written. Some similarities included three series fires, conducting surveillance on the suspect, setting fires during or along the way to fire investigator seminars and avoiding detection.

Meoli: As the investigation began, a novel was found entitled, "Points of Origin," which was penned by you. Authorities claimed that Aaron Stiles, the antagonist/arsonist within this fictional novel, was actually you. They pointed out many similarities and actions were very closely related to the arsonist who had committed the warehouse fires and others. Can you clarify this very important point?

Orr: "Aaron Stiles," the antagonist/protagonist in the manuscript was a composite of several real arsonists I had arrested or apprehended. He

25

did not have characteristics of myself. He did not have friends or close acquaintances, was never married, had difficulties with women and had trouble even at work. Unknown until now, (I share with you) there were several firefighters who attended arson investigation conferences, (some not registered), I felt uneasy about, and also fire personalities I came across in the Los Angeles area who were "wannabe" types. I felt fit the profile of "firebugs." Just an unease around them and I found them difficult to get to know. If you showed too much interest in them, they suddenly moved on.

Meoli: During one of our personal phone conversations, you stated you rarely encountered arsonists who were sexually aroused by watching their fires. If this is true, why does the fictional account of the arsonist, (on page 86 of "Points of Origin"), describe Aaron Stiles in the following manner - "He relaxed and partially closed the door, pulling the zipper down on his pants. He reached in, stroked his erection and watched the fire." Why the discrepancy?

Orr: The fact I rarely encountered a sexually motivated arsonist creates a discrepancy with how I portrayed Aaron in "Points of Origin." Lay people, when they encounter an authority describing how an arsonist actually gets aroused around fires, find this baffling and usually states, "That's bullshit." It is hard to believe.

My training sessions devoted little time to case histories about such motivations because there are few studied – it is rare. However, in 1980 I went through fire department archives and found a case from the 1950's, in Glendale, reporting an actual sexually motivated pyro.

They cops and firemen called him "Walleye," because he had one eye that had a life all its own, along with other maladies, (physical and emotional), contributing to his oddities. He set a series of *fires, including burning paper in a trash can or sink while watching his girlfriend have sex with another man.

It was fascinating to read, however, a real case. The guy confessed completely. Also, my writing instructor (Les Roberts) taught us to make your characters memorable, the bad guys downright weird, and guess what – sex sells, even perverted sex, according to Les. So, I complied. "Aaron" from several real sources became real in my tale. Besides, isn't fiction making up crap?

*Downtown alley fires in trash areas, cars and bushes/grass.

Meoli: Throughout "Points of Origin," there are large amounts of sexually driven dialogue (including male ejaculation during sex) and a heavy use of profanity. What was your reason for including such descriptive sexuality if you felt that arsonists are rarely sexually driven?

Orr: This answer is similar to the previous one. I wasn't writing porn, but while penning Aaron's scenes, I spoke his words and described his actions vividly because they were in character for him, albeit in third person.

Meoli: In your novel, "Points of Origin," you detailed how "Aaron Stiles" (the fictional arsonist) attended annual fire investigator conferences, (page 73), which was one of the main ways that investigators narrowed their search for a suspect. How do you explain this eerie similarity?

Orr: I started "Points of Origin" without an outline, just a basic concept of a fireman-gone-bad. As I have said before, I've met several firemen at conferences who stood off by themselves and did not fit in – loners. I went as far as getting one guy's name, (my sixth sense), on a pretext and later checked registration – he did not register, nor pay for enrollment, yet simply attended sessions. Whether he/they were just cheap or did not want a record they were in the area, I noted this phenomenon and later incorporated it in "Points of Origin." My novel was based on "what I know" and I pursued the fictional investigation as I would a real-life case. In around 1990, the organizations also notified the "no pays" and tightened up requirements and enforced a strict badge-entry registration.

Meoli: During the arson investigation, the unidentified subject (unsub) was dubbed the "Pillow Pyro." Who provided this moniker and why is this name relevant to the incendiary devices that were being found?

Orr: The "Pillow Pyro" fires were pillows and other polyurethane type ignition locations/origins that the incendiary devices were placed upon. I believe the moniker came from the Los Angeles Fire Department's Arson Unit who had many of these fires in 1990-1991. The devices comprised of a cigarette and a Band-Aid as I recall. Both wooden and paper matches were used. In fact, the fingerprint device had wooden matches where most recoveries were with book matches. Both filtered and unfiltered cigarettes were employed.

Meoli: What specific materials made up the "time-delay incendiary devices" that were being found?

Orr: As stated previously, the devices were comprised of a cigarette and a Band-Aid. Wooden and paper matches were used. Both filtered and unfiltered cigarettes were also employed.

Meoli: Who were the agencies, individuals or detectives that drove the investigation towards you as being the "Pillow Pyro?"

Orr: The Los Angeles Fire Department and the Bureau of Alcohol, Tobacco and Firearms (BATF).

Meoli: One of the most damning articles of evidence was a fingerprint found on a piece of paper after one of the fires. Therefore the arsonist had to have been at the scene of the crime before the fire began. How do you explain your fingerprint being found on the paper near the incendiary device?

Orr: When the paper was found, it was only after ninhydrin was applied that the print became visible or observable. The print is probably a legitimate print, just not mine. The paper was the same type and dimensions as those found in the registration notebook, (the gift provided to each attendee on the days prior to the fire) – it could have been innocently touched.

Meoli: Was the fingerprint that was found immediately linked to you at the time or was there some form of enhancement?

Orr: The found print (January 1987) was run through the state AFIS computer with no match found. It was a viable (8-9 points) print when found, so no enhancements were necessary. After another, similar series of fires in 1989, the still excellent print, (now a photograph), was again submitted, without enhancements, through AFIS – again no match and a list of 11 suspects, including myself, were compared. There was still no *match. It was not until another series of fires, 250 miles away, and two years later, that the print was re-examined and a Los Angeles County Sheriff's "expert" decided there were gaps or incomplete whorls that needed enhancing. He added lines and ran the enhanced print through AFIS and got a hit – mine and nine others, with me listed first.

*A supervisory lab tech also examined/compared the prints and signed off as "no match."

Meoli: Who performed the fingerprint enhancement and why was this deemed necessary with 8-9 points of reference?

Orr: A Los Angeles County Sheriff's lab tech decided there were gaps in the photograph of the original print and traced the photo-print onto plain paper, then added the connections he felt appropriate.

Meoli: Was there any other forensic evidence that linked you to these serial fires?

Orr: None.

Meoli: Do you have an alibi, (meaning it would have been physically impossible for you to have been on scene), for any of the fires for which you were alleged to have committed?

Orr: Alibi: The Prosecution's blanket theory was that I was responsible for all Los Angeles' area retail fires, including the "chip fires." I was the "Pillow Pyro" and the "Frito Bandito." Many of these "uncharged acts" were allowed as evidence in my trials after evidentiary hearing's testimony by a few expert witnesses stated that retail-open-for-business fires were "rare" and one person was responsible for all of them.

     My lawyers stated, "We will sandbag our alibi fires and ambush them in trial to refute their claims..." I blared back, "If we do not refute their experts at this hearing, we may convince the judge to not allow "uncharged acts." We have several solid alibis for "uncharged acts..." The lawyers refused and the judge ruled, "I will allow the twenty (20) 'uncharged acts'...and entertain more later." Over 100 were later presented in discovery. This alone proved such fires were far from "rare," but my lawyers had other ideas and they also said, "Some of the alibi 'uncharged acts' are not on the prosecutor's radar...we do not want to then bring in more. Let's see how it goes."

One alibi fire on April 4, 1975, at an Ole's (same company outlet as the 1984 fatal fire), store in the San Fernando Valley area of Los Angeles, started in polyurethane products and was included on the task force's list of fires. Unknown to them, I was on vacation in Barstow, California (125 miles away), and have not only gas receipts for April 27, 1985, in Bartow, but photos of me and my wife, (and witnesses), at the fireman's annual Ghost Town camping trip.

My lawyers never presented this rebuttal/alibi despite having photos of the scene. Side-by-side with my camping trip photos proves my alibi – but it was an "uncharged act" (over 30% of the prosecution's witnesses and evidence were related to "uncharged acts").

On September 9, 1988 and September 25, 1988, there were fires in Garden Grove (Orange County, California), which is south of Los Angeles. These fires started in foam rubber products, one destroying the entire store, occurring while I was again, camping, with a video with dates and witnesses to prove this. I've already sent you an article where the actual arsonist confesses to these two "similar fires."

On January 31, 1989, at a fabric store in Fresno, CA, an arson attempt is discovered after someone stocking shelves smelled smoke. This was 2 weeks after the seminar where a series of retail fires occurred and I was subsequently charged with five of them. I was found not guilty of this particular fire despite our in-court defense agreeing that all of those fires were set by the same person. I was in Los Angeles at the time of this fire, some 250 miles away, which was a pretty good alibi. The "John Orr device" is recovered at this fire.

A "potato chip" rack fire on November 11, 1989, at a market in South Central Los Angeles occurred. I was on vacation. No device recovered. On May 28, 1991, a fire set at a grocery outlet in nearby San Gabriel, rubber products – no device recovered. I was involved in a Glendale Fire Department training session at the same time. On December 26, 1990, a series of three fires destroyed two retail stores around noon in Los Angeles, about 10 miles west of Glendale. I was on-duty that day, by myself, and I joined my partner for lunch about the time these fires occurred. A suspect was arrested for all three of these fires (and one other) and held for over 2 years. When I was arrested, we discovered he was seen at two of the locations, pre-fire, yet the charges were dropped after my arrest. No devices were found, but the fires started in foam rubber products. My only alibi was that I would never wander 10 miles out of my jurisdiction when I was the only on-call investigator. My partner stated I was with him.

October 10, 1984 – the Ole's Hardware Store fire and two "potato chip" fires. My time-line proves it was impossible to set all three of these fires as the prosecution presented at trial. Keep in mind in none of the charged crimes was an incendiary device recovered – none in the fatal fire cases in the Los Angeles trial. Despite experts determining that the Ole's fire was accidentally caused, the prosecution used "experts" and document/photo reviews only to determine, that 14 years later, Ole's was arson and I did it.

A civil jury in 1989, found the accidentally caused scenarios believable and awarded more than $1,000,000 in insurance damages. The judge in my criminal trial refused to allow my criminal jury to hear that. They rendered a verdict verifying it was an "accidental cause" – but the judge only allowed the fact there was a civil trial. The time-line is bulletproof!

Using prosecution witnesses and reports, their scenario of setting the 6:30pm "potato chip" fire and the Ole's fire, (at 8:00pm, some 7.5 miles away), is feasible, however, they also throw in another "chip" fire, a half mile south of Ole's at around 8:00pm. There is a prosecution witness who places me in a face-to-face meeting with him at the first "chip" fire at 8:00-8:05pm, 7 miles away. There is not enough time, in any scenario, to drive 7 miles, (after 8:05pm) and set two other fires. The only logical explanation is that Ole's was indeed accidentally caused.

Meoli: After your arrest, were any similar "time delay" device fires found in any warehouse or other similar fires in Glendale, California or surrounding areas?

Orr: Without research, it is not *possible to determine discovery of similar devices other than one found the day after my first conviction in Fresno, California. In custody 250 miles away, this cigarette/match device was recovered at a site that burned before and other devices were located. It was a real arsonist making a statement in Los Angeles while I was housed in a Fresno, California jail.

*Prosecutors and investigators were not motivated to provide us with such exculpatory information.

Meoli: You assert that you are innocent of these crimes. If this is true, why do you think you were named as a suspect?

Orr: I believe investigators reviewed a copy of my manuscript, "Points of Origin" and found the uncanny similarities to their real case too coincidental to believe. My fictional story used actual information from their real case, legitimately learned, with enhancements to dramatize the story. It was only then that detectives "enhanced" the fingerprint and declared it mine.

Meoli: Was there anything during your trial you feel was malpractice by your lawyer(s) or not brought to light that you would want the world to know?

Orr: Reference the time line for the most glaring ineptness of not presenting a valid alibi. Since there was no forensic evidence produced at the murder trial, my lawyers should have focused on the major charge and presented a 5' x 6' timeline to graphically show the jury that the prosecution's assertions were just wrong in the Ole's case. It was an accidentally-caused fire.

My lawyers did not search for a missing set of 35mm negatives that would refute another of the prosecution's theory to prove Ole's was an arson case: The pictures would show the first shots I took upon arrival to reveal fire through the roof of Ole's (see inset picture) after only 10-12 minutes of life. Prosecutors said the fire did not breach the roof quickly because it was arson and ignited at ground level inside the store.

Experts in 1982 suggested and determined the fire originated in a drop ceiling/attic area and burned through the roof structure. The prosecutor's statements and their experts said the fire took a longer time to burn through and provided only an incomplete set of 36 photos I took in 1984. The missing photos would match the sequence of the one photo (enclosed) clearly revealing fire-through-the-roof.

There may be two other pictures before that one to further complete the defense's theory. I demanded the negatives be presented to determine the sequence, but prosecutors said they couldn't find them. They were seized in a search warrant service on my office.

The through-the-roof theory was highlighted throughout my trial, yet my lawyers did not seek the missing photos or negatives. Post-trial, I found a reference in documents I had never seen before revealing two possible locations of my full set of photographs, with at least one set of negatives in police and or city attorney archives.

The day after the fire I brought back an extra set of negatives for South Pasadena's Fire/Police Departments. I am positive they still reside, at least, in the city attorney's Ole's fire files.

Additionally, in at least two instances, federal prosecutors withheld exculpatory evidence in the first trial. Three suspects, (one alone and a pair), were investigated for fires in Fresno that I was charged with, yet reports referring to these men were excised from discovery material. With a little due diligence, we may have discovered these hidden suspects. The pair appeared to have set fires as diversions to steal while the fires burned. One of this pair of arsonists was suspected of setting fires in the very Holiday Inn where the arson conferences were held. Local investigators hinted at these guys, but stonewalled the defense's efforts to research.

Eyewitnesses gave a similar description of the arsonist pair in the Fresno fires: "Disheveled looking, mid-20's guys with long hair and prominent whiskers." Both suspects' mug shots obtained by the defense revealed exact matches to witness identifications. At the time of the fires, I had a permanently receding hairline, was 38 years old, with a full beard, and wore glasses with short hair. We did not have these photographs or suspects until after the first trial.

The third suspect had priors: setting fires in open retail outlets as shoplifting diversions and was arrested just six blocks from a Salinas, California, fire location that I was accused of setting; in search/arrest warrants and affidavits. The guy's references were explicit in a three-page addendum to the Salinas Police Department, but those three pages were removed before discovery was given to the defense.

There were many in-trial failures by my lawyers in the murder trial, but three weeks before opening statements they told me, "We are out of money and the trial is expected to take 8-10 weeks, so we are in trial for free. John, take the deal." I did not, even though the death penalty would have been taken off the table. The prosecution put on 12 days, and the defense rested after 7 hours, not calling many credible witnesses nor presenting alibi evidence – they were in too much of a hurry.

Meoli: What does it feel like to have to live with the moniker, "The Most Prolific Serial Arsonist of the 20th Century?"

Orr: It is depressing to exist with that slur after dedicating 24 years to the fire service, fighting for everything I was accused of creating – fire. I later embraced the quote to help get my real story out in the form of my memoir: "Points of Truth – Revelations of the Most Prolific Serial Arsonist of the 20th Century."

Meoli: You penned "Points of Truth" (2010). What was the purpose of this book?

Orr: After years of being beaten down and watching documentaries fabricate and speculate fake facts, I decided I had to answer the slurs. I also read articles in magazines and references to me in true crime books where the same errors were made. Even when I provided my bulletproof alibi timeline and other exonerating alibis to a best-selling author writing about me, he basically ignored the true evidence.

I had to answer all the questions, even the case investigators never asked. I want them to know what they overlooked, answer their speculations about my "evasive counter surveillance moves" or where I actually was when they lost me and a fire occurred nearby – I had stepped into a conference room to give a presentation scheduled weeks in advance; they never queried me. I will still consent to an open interview with case investigators/prosecutors – bring it on!

Meoli: Do you feel that you will ever be found innocent of these crimes? If so, how?

Orr: Yes, I do, at least in the murder/arson case. My memoir is the primary reason I feel I have a chance, since all the alibis that were never presented are now exposed, as well as the insidious prosecutorial misconduct of concealing exonerating evidence. Simply put, if you are innocent then take the stand and be heard. The Ole's time line is truth.

Meoli: What would you want to do with the rest of your life if you were released from prison?

Orr: Total exoneration would result in my instructing others on criminal investigation procedures. Using my case as an example, I would focus on the unreliability of fire scene "clues" and how misread signs can create an arson. Mistaken identification is also a horrendous part of many cases and I can refute 60% of those false identifications of me used in my case investigation pre-trial. One such false identification of me by a police officer provided impetus to case investigators that they had the right man – me. But, I would provide a video of the encounter and the actual man to testify; it was he at the scene – not me. I would embrace teaching to help new investigators. Oh, and I would go to the beach!

Meoli: If there are any other points you would like to make, please feel free to share them here:

Orr: I have led a pretty exemplary life. My worth ethic was commendable since my first job at Jack-in-the-Box all the way to Fire Captain. I was never arrested, got along with everybody, was always a good neighbor, played "Secret Santa" for a few years and helped create better relationships between fire and police investigators by providing specialized training for 10 years.

While I could have made better choices when I was in my early 20's, my defense of that time was that there were no classes in school on how to deal with relationships, your children, and the concept of responsibility. I should have focused more on my family life and my wives and children – but didn't. I put work, career and providing for my family as top priorities, when more time should have been focused on the family unit.

I later learned responsibility, but it took a while. If I had a bit more insight early on, I would have realized my Dad and Mom set an excellent example: Both worked to provide, but they also nurtured our family and produced some pretty decent and successful sons. I have not got a passel of enlightened and prospering children and grandchildren, but had hoped to be a better example to them.

Before I was arrested I had a great life and my abilities to deal with adversity now extend in prison. I try to exist in here using my prior life as a guide and I believe I can be called a "model prisoner." Meeting all my milestones to lower custody/security levels on time and sometimes well in advance. I have only one minor write up in 25 years in prison.

I live in here like I did outside – anything I do in here reflects on how I am perceived "out there" and I do not want to bring any more grief to law enforcement and the fire service than has already been done. I arrested over 150 individuals, over 40 of them serial fire setters. Nobody remembers the successes, advancements, and positive contributions I made. I am proud of my life and despite my predicament, hold my head high.

Orr's Statement regarding his Guilty Plea Bargain

I was innocent of the Fresno charges but was convicted on three of the five counts against me. My attorney (Giannini) advised me that there was either little or no grounds for appeal to succeed. The cost of defending two cases eliminated all resources available to me. The Fresno trial devastated my family, friends and the Glendale Fire Department.

I did not want any of us to go through the trauma of another trial. I was weakened by the wrongful conviction and I did not have the financial ability to hire private investigators to interview potential witnesses. I knew these witnesses would confirm my alibi documentation on five of the eight counts.

These witnesses were never interviewed by attorney Giannini and the $60,000 fee did not include the cost of hiring a private investigator. The remaining three counts were the Atascadero, California fires and only I could testify to the fact that I was forty to fifty miles south of Atascadero at the times of these fires.

I spoke with two people during that day but a private investigator would spend many hours to search for these witnesses who may not even remember the contact four years after the fact. But I could not testify without impeachment and introduction of the erroneous Fresno conviction at the Los Angeles trial. So, with the guarantee of no further jail time in the plea agreement, I accepted the deal.

Also we know that the Los Angeles District Attorney's Office was investigating a number of other arson fires including the fatal Ole's blaze in 1984 (although this was declared an accidental fire and over $4,000,000 was successfully recovered by the heirs of the deceased based on an electrical malfunction in the attic). I asked my lawyer about the effect of pleading guilty in the federal case on future cases if the Los Angeles District Attorney filed any new charges.

The plea bargain on page six clearly said and with my attorney's reassurance that there was no jeopardy. Unfortunately, the Los Angeles (Builder's Emporium fire) I pleaded guilty to experienced a previous arson fire just 3 days after the 10-10-1984 Ole's fire.

We chose the North Hollywood fire because there was only $60 in damage and the rest of the Los Angeles fires had higher damages or carried potential civil ramifications. Pleading guilty to this fire opened the door for the Los Angeles District Attorney to file their cases and even though a plea bargain says it cannot be used – it is being done to allow the jury to hear I said I was guilty of setting fires similar to the fatal Ole's fire.

The prosecution in the federal case withheld their knowledge of the 1984 Builder's Emporium, North Hollywood fire, along with many others. The Los Angeles District Attorney is now depending on the coerced guilty pleading as "evidence" that "Orr did it all," including the fatal fire at Ole's despite clear evidence in the Ole's case that it was impossible for Orr to have been involved. This information is in District Attorney Cabral's possession yet he is prosecuting and relying on these errors. Obviously he expected me to cop a plea in the Los Angeles case. He is wrong.

The Evidence

(Original photographs with comments provided by John Orr)

Figure 1: John Orr arriving on scene, taken the evening of October 10, 1984

This original photo is said to be extremely important for his defense case. This was the third or fourth photo taken by Orr on the evening of October 10, 1984. This fire would eventually take the lives of four people and be the murder case that would eventually sentence him to life in prison without the possibility of parole.

Orr sent this picture along with many others to follow that were intended to explain his version of a timeline that he states would have made it virtually impossible for him to have set this fatal fire. His explanation was that he was meeting Scott McClure (witness) of Pasadena, California.

Orr says it is important to note when looking at the fire - it is already burning through the roof and refutes the trial-long assertion by prosecutors during his trial, that the fire originated on the sales floor, not in the drop-ceiling or attic space as determined by numerous fire investigators in 1984.

Orr states the two full fire hose lines, (seen in the background in front of the concrete wall) and the state of the hose being pulled from the bed of this engine, (unknown fire company) pinpoint the timing to some degree. Orr's states his lawyers never pursued this angle during his defense trial.

The photos taken before this particular scene allegedly show Orr's car and other factors that would confirm his arrival time along with the allegation by Orr, that this fire originated in the attic space and breeched/burned through the roof early on. This clearly differed from the prosecution's theory that this was similar to the methods employed by the serial arsonist which investigators had narrowed in on during that time in 1984.

Figure 2: Orr's Cardura Bag

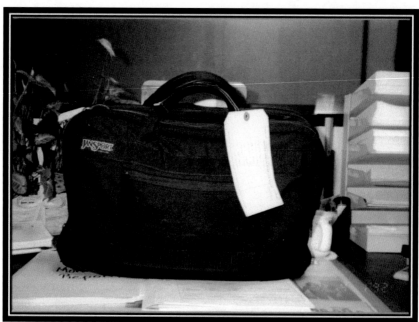

This is another original photo, note time stamp on the lower right corner (see Figure 2), which details the Jansport bag investigators found when searching John Orr's residence. The contents within the bag are described in vivid detail on the back of each photo on the ensuing pages.

Orr dismisses some of the evidence as being commonly found items that would be discovered in anyone's bag if searched. It is not so much as what is found as how Orr describes the items that gives them context. He appears content that none of the evidence is overtly incriminating and willfully sent these pictures to be copied.

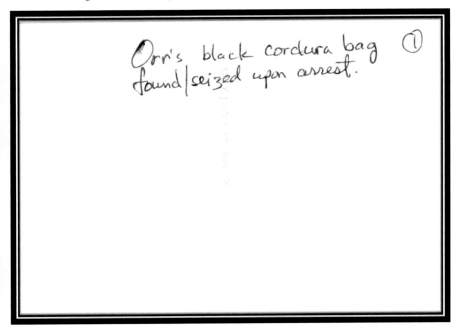

Orr commenting on the verso of the "black bag." Orr admits within this interview that he had no idea that he was a suspect in the serial fires until the day he was arrested. He appears oblivious to the fact that investigators were not only tracking his movements with a GPS attached to his car, but even proposes the idea that it could have been a game investigators were playing. He also admits it could have been the "feds" looking at him.

John Orr repeatedly speaks about the rule of law when admitting guilt or having evidence found. He does not deny that fact that an innocent person would not have any such evidence, their fingerprint or a manuscript that proposed the very time delay device that was used by the arsonist in the serial fires.

Figure 3: Items from Compartment #1 of Orr's Cardura Bag

Compartment #1   ④

1) evidence collection plastic bags
2) bandana for general use and to wipe inside of dusty
   car's windshield — subject to fogging
3) Black dashboard cover — to kill the sun's reflection
   off the shiny dashboard which made driving difficult.
4) incense sticks — to nullify fire-scene-transferred smoke
   smells brought in on clothes after investigations.
5) Rubber bands for generic use including to hold incense stick
   in place on transmission shifter, sealing plastic bags, etc.
6) Rocks, weights used in week-long investigation class 10
   days before arrest — extra rubber bands for class use, too
7) Velcro for generic use.
8) Cigs and lighter for "softening" up suspects in interrogations.
   (Brand did not match those found in '90-'91 fires.
9) Corkscrew for spontaneous post-dinner evenings out
10) Day-planner

Figure 4: Items from Compartment #2 of Orr's Cardura Bag

2 - zippered sides   ③
Generic day-to-day necessities
1) Dept. and personal keyrings — single key
   to FD gas pumps/fire road locks.
2) Pentax mini-binoculars
3) Evidence phone conversation cassette (or
   maybe Vivaldi's Four Seasons?

Figure 5: Items from Compartment #3 (2 of 2 Zippered Sides), of Orr's Cardura Bag

1) More evidence bags (plastic under the paper bags) ⑤
2) off-duty job as PI folder for forms, timesheets

In this particular description, Orr explains how he suddenly had an off-duty job as a private investigator. There is no record to support that Orr ever was licensed as a private investigator in the State of California, nor any business associated to him in this capacity. Orr may have worked in this capacity, but given his limited education, the fact that he was not a police officer, and was never registered as a private investigator, this seems more like yet another excuse to explain away items being found.

Figure 6: Close-up of Orr's folder with the photo of a GPS tracking device that was placed under his bumper

Close-up of off-duty folder also ⑦ showing photos I took of the tracking device on my car in May 1991 in San Luis Obispo. I also made 2-4 fingerprint lifts from the bumper and inside my car and transferred them to 3"x5" cards. I theorized the feds slim-jimmed my car and made entry late one night while tailing me (outlined in PoT). The print cards went missing after arrest — probably trashed by the very agents who entered my car without a warrant.

It is interesting to note how much effort John Orr puts into explaining away the tracking device found on his car. In a self-described chain of events, Orr admits, "The feds slim-jimmed my car and made entry late one night while tailing me." The idea was that fingerprint cards were made, then went missing – thereby being unable to be proven by Orr. These were made by the same agents who entered his car without a warrant – yet no proof existed of actual entry. The only evidence was the placement of the tracking device (See Figure 6).

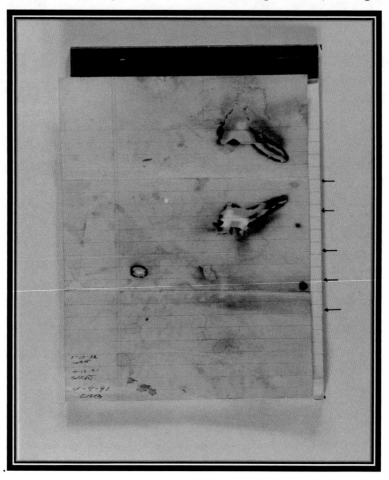

Figure 7: Yellow lined paper showing remnants of Time-Delay Device

John Orr states this "yellow lined paper" (YLP), shows remnants of a timed-delay type of device and therefore, is considered evidence - wherein a partial fingerprint (matching Orr's) was found. The fingerprint was not perfect, meaning that the Automated Fingerprint Identification System (AFIS) did not initially detect a perfect match.

Initially, eleven suspects (see Figure 8 for suspect list, Orr is #5) were "inked" by the California Department of Justice, all with negative results. After Orr's fingerprint was enhanced, meaning someone physically traced/drew over portions of his partial print, it came back as a "match."

The following statement by Orr explains the importance of the YLP evidence.

Orr: The yellow lined paper (YLP) with burn damage photo did contain the cigarette/match type delayed device which was also recovered, but I do not have those photos. As I recall, the "fingerprint/YLP device" comprised of a filtered cigarette and wooden matches. The cigarette filter itself was also subjected to ninhydrin and revealed a faint print, yet unreadable for classification purposes. Though DNA was in its infancy in 1987, (maybe an embryo as I recall), the case investigator threw away the device components while retaining the YLP.

There was a $100,000 fire shortly after the YLP/Print fire, (an hour later), in a fabric store on the same side of Bakersfield,

California. No said device found, yet Investigator Casey tossed out a major piece of evidence, less than a month into the statute of limitations to retain crime evidence (3 years minimum at a time to retain evidence). If Casey were to have identified a suspect in the YLP fire, the type of cigarette, the type of wooden matches and maybe even the rubber band remnants could have been compared to items in a suspect's possession – but they all went in the trash. I do not know if today's technology in fingerprint identification is any more advanced than it was in 1987-1991, but maybe the print on that discarded cigarette could or could not be "enhanced."

Just to be clear, the damaged YLP overlaying the full pad of YLP with 5 arrows (inked onto the photo) staged after my 12-4-1991, arrest, and after the chain of custody (dates and initials) on the lower left quadrant of the YLP. On 01/20/1992, the evidence was in possession of the BATF task force in Los Angeles and Fresno, pre-trial (1992). The pad on the bottom had impressions/marks where the inked arrows are pointing and possibly was one of several seized during the search warrant service on my home/office.

As I recall, statements by investigators said there were similar marks/impressions on the edges of the damaged YLP. I do not know what they were trying to prove by comparing a piece of YLP from the 1987, (the fingerprint YLP), to a random pad I used from my office supply closet in 1991, when arrested 4 years later. The margin marks/impressions comparison was a "wash" and appeared a characteristic in the manufacturing process, storage, or packaging – especially on samples from 4 years apart. The similarities were

57

presented in court with an actual pad manufacturer confirming nothing but speculation of marks from the manufacturer, transportation packaging, etc. It held no forensic value and it was still thrown out in court as a red herring.

CALIFORNIA DEPARTMENT OF JUSTICE
DIVISION OF LAW ENFORCEMENT
BUREAU OF FORENSIC SERVICES

FRESNO REGIONAL CRIMINALISTICS LABORATORY

6014 NORTH CEDAR, FRESNO 93710

To:
Alcohol, Tobacco and Firearms
1130 O Street
Fresno, CA 93721

Copies To:

Attention: Special Agent Charles Galyan

PHYSICAL EVIDENCE EXAMINATION REPORT

TYPE OF CASE	REQUESTING AGENCY	
451 P.C.	Alcohol Tobacco and Firearms	
SUBJECT		
Russell BUSH		
EXHIBITS RECEIVED FROM	DATE	TIME
Special Agent Galyan	4-3-89	
METHOD OF TRANSIT		
In Person		

This is a report concerning physical evidence examinations requested by your office. In any future correspondence regarding this case please use the BFS case number appearing at the top of this report.

The undersigned, a Latent Print Analyst employed by the State of California, if called as a witness, would testify, under penalty of perjury, that he/she did perform the examinations, tests and analyses necessary to reach the findings, opinions and conclusions stated below.

SUMMARY:

The usable impression appearing in the submitted photograph was compared with the inked fingerprints of eleven subjects with negative results.

EVIDENCE AND INDICATED SOURCE:

1. Photographic negative marked 3-11-87 CAS
2. Photograph of latent impression marked 3-11-89 CAS

On 4-13-89 the Latent Print program submitted the machine copies of the inked fingerprints of the following subjects:

1. Russel BUSH
2. James LONZCAK
3. Steven DALE
4. Robert TINKER
5. John ORR
6. Patrick SMOLLEN
7. Larry TITUS
8. James FORTE
9. Richard KELLY
10. Gary GLENN

Continued

Date of Report:........................   Examinations by: ....

Title:.....................................:..........................

Figure 8: Physical Evidence Examinations Report Placing John Orr at #5

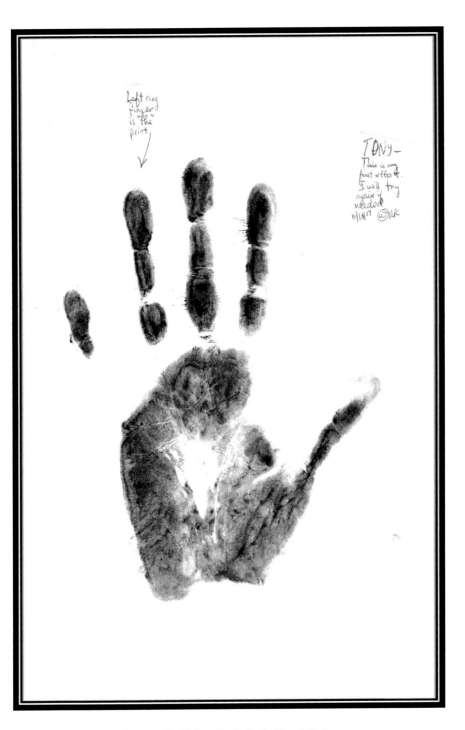

Figure 9: John Orr's Left-Hand Print

60

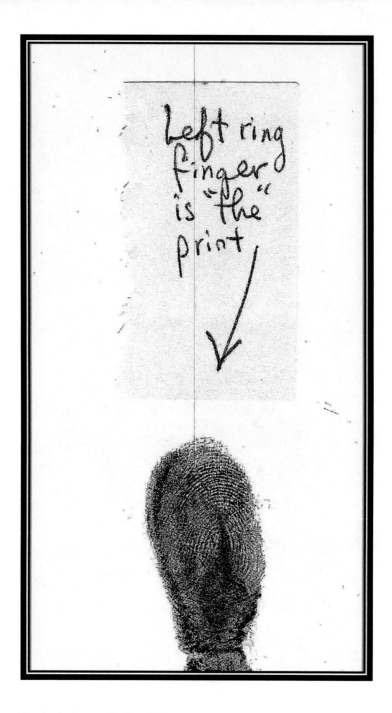

Figure 10: Orr's Magnified Left Ring Finger Print. Orr's comments on how this particular finger was the one that convicted him.

This is the actual left handprint of John Orr. Here, Orr details his ring finger that would become the center of focus of the serial fire investigations.

I had requested a full palm print from him in order to get an idea of what his fingerprints would look like as opposed to a latent print that had to be "enhanced" before detection. Additionally, many years ago and even today, full handprints were rarely taken in most jurisdictions. In some cases, the only evidence is partial finger or palm prints. Thus, my request. Below is John Orr's response to said request.

Meoli: Do you fully understand my request for a full palm print?

Orr: I think you are correct and do not recall them taking my palm print twenty-five years ago. I had my prints taken every time I moved into a new jail/prison/holding facility, but do not ever recall a full handprint being taken. I agree with you that having a full palm print is important (included in this letter) because it could lead to undiscovered evidence, should they have a partial palm print related to the fires.

Also, as you remember from our letters and "Points of Truth," the AFIS computer did spit out ten (10) suspects when they ran the enhanced photo of the YLP print. I do not recall this as typical but I never was involved in the AFIS computer. In my day, you gave the print to somebody – they ran it – and got back to you later (just a state computer as I remember).

Figure 11: Orr's Final Addendum Notes

Final addendum notes for this interview from Orr. He admits to "setting about 100 fires" during training sessions for investigators. This is related to an August 1982 article written for the Western Fire Journal. The title is not nearly as interesting as the article's contents nor its authors.

"Working to Solve Arson's Epidemic" was written by John Orr and Dennis Wilson, both fire investigators. While his note (Figure 11) is supported by the article in that several fires were intentionally set, under controlled conditions, with donated structures - a few odd revelations appear.

On page 2 of this particular article, it speaks of a "homemade destructive/incendiary device." Probably the most interesting aspects of this entire article are the details of the device and the date.

I was slightly surprised this article was not brought up at trial, since the date of the article precedes the 1984 Ole's fatal fire by a full two years. What is of most interest appears on page 3 of this article (Figure 16). In searching for more information about this particular fire journal article, I did not this article cited in any legal case, textbook, or other reference prior to John Orr sending it to me for this publication.

WORKING TO SOLVE ARSON'S EPIDEMIC

EXECUTIVE SUMMARY

Fire and police personnel join forces to combat arson through innovative inter-departmental training in Glendale, California.

By JOHN ORR &
DENNIS WILSON
Fire Investigators, City of
Glendale (California)

The growing arson problem has forced most municipalities to take a long hard look at their abilities and capabilities to handle this serious problem.

The City of Glendale, California (population 140,000), was no exception and in November, 1980 a joint fire/police arson task force was formed. One police officer and one firefighter were selected, trained and

curred at 1 A.M. and the investigators were not called to the scene. The following day, through routine checking of the previous days fire calls, the investigators learned of the incident. Witnesses who were at the scene of the fire had to be tracked down and extra manhours were spent developing the case. As a result, the juvenile fled to Michigan one day before a search warrant was issued for his residence where important evidence was seized.

As a result, the investigators submitted a training proposal to the fire and police department staffs in an effort to help alleviate the problems. In the proposal the investigators outlined

ways asked regarding city liability, safety and, of course, cost.

The investigators volunteered two weekends of their time, the structures were donated, and only $45.00 worth of supplies were needed. Approval of the city's legal department was already granted and the city safety officer offered his time for on-site safety during the burning. The fire department staff gave their approval in mid-February.

Old furniture was obtained from Goodwill Industries of Los Angeles as well as from the cleaning out of the investigators' own garages.

Since the structures were in a re-development area, security of the vacant

assigned to work exclusively in fire arson investigation.

Shortly after its inception, it became apparent to the investigators that this new addition to the city's safety services had growing pains. Lack of initial media exposure, as well as inter-departmental communications, soon showed that many citizens as well as members of both the police and fire departments were unaware of the team's existence and/or functions. Thus, several early cases were jeopardized by the team not being notified or being called in well after the incident.

One example was a juvenile being identified as responsible for several burglaries and an arson fire. The arson and a burglary of several vehicles oc-

the various difficulties and offered a remedy for the situation that would not create any outward criticisms or expose exact past incidents.

Five structures had been donated in a re-development area and the investigators asked that they be allowed to stage typical accidental and arson type fires in the buildings. The fires would be extinguished and later the fire companies would be shown through each "set" what took place. The fires would be set and allowed to burn only far enough to create significant char and burn patterns and then be extinguished cautiously to preserve "evidence."

Further explanation of the proposal provided the answers ultimately al-

buildings was vital. Though the city's liability was limited to the week of the session, the investigators chose to seal the buildings and make periodic checks to maintain their preservation, freeing the developer from that obligation. Nevertheless, breakins were common during the four weeks taken to prepare and even during the exercise. Some doors, hardware and furnishings were stolen and several windows were broken.

Original plans called for 10 scenes to include two vehicle fires and two outdoor fires (Molotov cocktail and a homemade destructive device).

Plans went smoothly for an early April training session until mid-

Continued on next page

100917

Figure 12: Orr and Wilson's Article, Page 1

ARSON . . .

March. A sudden increase in fires in Glendale and an injury to one investigator slowed progress. Numerous volunteers came forward from the fire departments of Glendale and Burbank as well as from the Glendale Police Department. But soon things were back on schedule.

Saturday morning, March 28, several companies of the Glendale Fire Department assisted in placing the furnishings in the structures and hanging draperies. Junk vehicles arrived and were secured.

Sunday morning, the session got underway with local TV and newspaper reporters in attendance. Our "secret" location did not last long as passersby and neighbors converged on the scene.

All the "scenes" were to be ignited by means of the most commonly used substances and devices used by "everyday" arsonists. The only exotic set was a homemade destructive/incendiary device.

What was supposed to start the day off spectacularly turned into a dismal failure when, after four attempts to detonate the device, the investigators only managed to set a mattress on fire accidentally.

Undeterred, the investigators moved on to a bedroom scene only to find a mattress had been stolen during the night. The mattress was not particularly vital to the scene and the arson fire was ignited. This scene involved igniting candles as a delayed timing device as well as crumpled newspapers as boosters. The fire burned spectacularly igniting a styrofoam ice chest and spreading to curtains and ultimately extinguished itself in the closed room. This was ideal since the investigators wanted to keep evidence as intact as possible for the Glendale fire crews to view during the following week. However, it was not to be this time either. One investigator had purchased DRIPLESS candles and the evidence literally went up in smoke, leaving no waxy residue. It was interesting to note this for future reference, and the investigators began leaning a few things, too.

The session continued rather smoothly with approximately 30 attempts at igniting furnishings, cars and trash with cigarettes. Only one of these attempts was successful. They had hoped to further explode the myth that cigarettes can be blamed for a majority of fires. Granted, they are responsible for many fires, but today's modern synthetics are not nearly as susceptible to accidental ignition as those of years ago.

The only successful smoulder we produced was in a 20-year-old, overstuffed couch. After the cigarette was dropped between the cushion and armrest, only five minutes was needed for a sizable burn pattern to develop. Inside 15 minutes, the small bedroom was untenable with smoke approaching the floor level. The door was closed and after *four hours* less than half the couch was involved. No open flame was apparent until the door was opened. Flames then enveloped the entire couch and the fire crew had to back out and re-group before re-entering and extinguishing the fire. (A backdraft condition had nearly developed, but, for safety reasons, the room was entered and extinguishment affected.)

All scenes were documented with before, during and after photographs to better demonstrate to the firefighters what had occurred and to enable them to recognize signs they had seen in past fires as well as to ready them for fires they will see in the future. The investigators are currently developing a slide show to be used in training new firefighters and as a refresher course for in-service personnel.

A side-by-side bedroom scene with nearly identical furnishings was used next. Gasoline was distributed throughout the interior of one room and ignited by means of a flare thrown into the room. (A half-gasoline-half-30-wt.-oil mixture was used to cut down on fume development for safety reasons and to produce better spill patterns.) The original intent in this set was to show the differences in a thorough overhaul job that ends up with vital evidence being put in a pile outside the structure and an efficient overhaul job that not only insures the fire is out but also saves the evidence. Once again plans were altered. After the first fire was extinguished, the investigators and crews decided that the sparsely-furnished room would have been left pretty much as it was in an actual fire situation. The remaining evidence was readily visible and was

100948

Figure 13: Orr and Wilson's Article Page 2

ARSON . . .

March. A sudden increase in fires in Glendale and an injury to one investigator slowed progress. Numerous volunteers came forward from the fire departments of Glendale and Burbank as well as from the Glendale Police Department. But soon things were back on schedule.

Saturday morning. March 28, several companies of the Glendale Fire Department assisted in placing the furnishings in the structures and hanging draperies. Junk vehicles arrived and were secured.

Sunday morning. the session got underway with local TV and newspaper reporters in attendance. Our "secret" location did not last long as passersby and neighbors converged on the scene.

All the "scenes" were to be ignited by means of the most commonly used substances and devices used by "everyday" arsonists. The only exotic set was a homemade destructive/incendiary device.

Figure 14: Orr and Wilson's Article Page 2 Enlargement

The blown-up section of page 2 of Orr's article shown in full on the previous page. The article goes on to state, "the only exotic set was a homemade destructive/incendiary device" (Figure 14). It is not until page 3 of this article where details of what materials made up this "homemade device" are divulged.

demonstrated the initial flame colors of flammable liquid involvement and their change to the common combustible colors as the gasoline was consumed and burned away. Spill patterns and low burning along baseboards and furnishings also developed. The flare residue was readily apparent in the first set but was considerably more difficult to recognize in the second. The flare ended up below a chest of drawers with numerous cosmetics and miscellaneous objects on it, and the flare looked very much like a tube of toothpaste until it was turned over to expose the waxy, red casing.

A small, fully-furnished two-bedroom house was used next. By this time, the police half of the arson unit was "chomping at the bit" to get involved in the extinguishment of a fire. Officer Wilson, in full protective gear, donned a breathing apparatus and stood by as his partner ignited the house by means of a cigarette-matchbook delay device and newspaper "trailers." The living room was fully involved in eight minutes as an 1½" line was advanced to the front door. In typical police fashion, Officer Wilson

Candle, placed on the bottom of a styrofoam ice chest, acts as a wick for delayed ignition at the scene of an arson fire.

Once the candle burns down, the ice chest ignites and quickly bursts into flame, setting the room on fire.

preserved despite a necessary aggressive attack on the extremely hot fire.

The companion bedroom scene was burned similarly, but using twice as much gasoline. The color photographs taken during this phase graphically

kicked in the front door only to be confronted with a wall of thick grey smoke to the floor level. Undeterred, Wilson entered standing straight up. As he disappeared into the smoke he was

Continued on next page

Western Fire Journal — August 1982   21

Figure 15: Orr and Wilson's Article Page 3

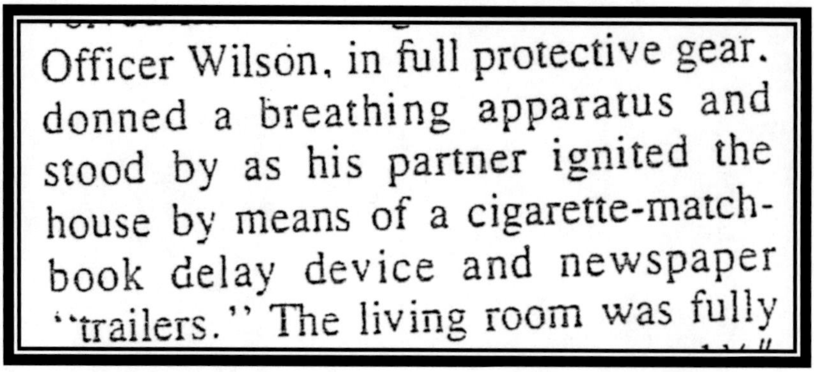

> Officer Wilson, in full protective gear.
> donned a breathing apparatus and
> stood by as his partner ignited the
> house by means of a cigarette-match-
> book delay device and newspaper
> "trailers." The living room was fully

Figure 16: Orr and Wilson's Article Page 3 Enlargement

This paragraph appears on page 3 of Orr's article. This 1982 article not only mentions the "homemade device" but its true make-up. The article goes on to specify that it is Wilson's partner, John Orr, "ignited the house by means of a cigarette-match book delay device and newspaper trailers." This is the exact type of incendiary device that would be found two years later in groups of serial fires and continue to be found until Orr's arrest.

CONCLUSION

While agreeing to remain open-minded, I found the 1982 article (previously unreferenced) to be incriminating on many fronts. First, the article was co-written by John Orr. Next, the incendiary device mentioned within this article was too close in time to the fires being set – under two years. Third, the construction of the homemade device was extremely similar to the Fresno, California and "Pillow Pyro" serial arson fires. Lastly, the article predates Orr's fictional manuscript and the aforementioned "chip fire" in Glendale.

What remains from this seemingly harmless article was that Orr had already developed the incendiary device. The device was "field tested" and worked well, setting various structures ablaze during these "100" controlled training fires.

While Orr vehemently asserts his innocence throughout this interview, it is nearly impossible to ignore the circumstantial evidence that is at the core of his conviction. For example, when trying to explain away the fact that a global positioning system (GPS) tracking device was placed underneath his vehicle – he described how this could have been a joke played by fellow investigators. However, Orr also refutes this idea by saying this device was placed without a warrant, so again there are two differing stories. One in that it was a joke that an extremely experienced serial arson fire task force was playing as a means to pass time, and the other that federal investigators, searching without a warrant, had not only placed the device but obtained his fingerprints from inside the car. All of this seem to be odd assumptions made by a seasoned former Chief Fire Investigator.

Orr's actions become increasingly alarming as the serial arsonist was narrowed down to eleven suspects. It is very important to note that none of the other suspects' fingerprints matched the partial fingerprint. There is no doubt that the fingerprint "enhancement" did take place, but this was performed later in time. The other suspects were only included because the "Pillow Pyro" task force had reduced the suspect list down to those fire investigators who had attended specific fire investigation seminars where serial fires had followed.

The enhanced fingerprint came back as a "hit" to only John Leonard Orr. His alibis for many of the fires are non-verifiable, with most involving either camping trips or meetings. If there was an arson related fire that did take place, John Orr was only a few miles away at the time or merely "camping."

Orr suffered with relationships throughout his life, including his own children. He had an uncommon difficulty (four divorces) with women. While some of his explanations for these divorces are rational, none of his marriages ever exceeded eight years. Most of his marriages failed before four years.

The 1984 photograph places John Orr at the scene taking photographs, watching the fire. None of the photos he provided showed that he was investigating the fire. While he may have some as indicated in his descriptions, these were never forwarded to my attention.

The original photograph (see Figure 1) sent by Orr clearly shows the fire appearing in the lower windows. This refutes his own claims that it was an electrical fire with the origin taking place mainly on the upper floors or roof of the structure.

It is clear that there are many similarities within his manuscript "Points of Origin" that coincide with the serial fires being investigated at the time. During one of our phone conversations, Orr admitted that in all the cases he had ever investigated, only two arsonists stuck out as ever being "sexually motivated" to commit their crimes. Orr readily admits that the inclusion of a strong, sexually motivated arsonist was a major discrepancy in his book from reality. The fictional antagonist, "Aaron Stiles," was a narcissistically, deviant, sexually motivated, serial arsonist. Stiles was compelled to curse, dehumanize women and even watch his fires to the point of masturbation.

Orr stated that this information was included in his manuscript to make his antagonist appear "weird." He also asserted that "sex sells." His explanation for all of this was due to a fictional writing instructor's directive. The information included within his manuscript mirrored the ongoing investigation far too closely. As with most serial arsonists, "Aaron Stiles" enjoyed watching his own fires grow and do more damage. As his own book states, the fires "provided him with feelings of importance and recognition."

Orr presented evidence of a timeline that should have put him too far away to have committed all three fires on October 10, 1984. However, he backtracks from this by admitting within this interview that it was "still possible" for him to have been present at two of the serial fire locations that evening. His lone defense was that there was simply not enough time to also be at the fatal fire location, proving it had to have been an electrical fire. Taking into account the odds that three serial arson fires took place on one night - the odds that two other fires were unrelated to the Ole's fire is difficult to believe.

Orr spoke about the hoses and lines and how this related to a timeline and electrical fire which would have been located much higher, near the roofline. However, when looking at the photograph, there is ample visual evidence that the lower floors show fire emanating from the windows. The 1984 Ole's fire is extremely important because it took four innocent lives. It is this original photographic evidence that places Orr at the scene, watching it burn.

John Orr admitted that the civil trial ruled the Ole's fire was "accidental" due to it being an electrical fire. This is only a partially true statement. What it ignores is that the point of origin was near an area of the building that an experienced serial arsonist and fire investigator would have found highly vulnerable. An argument could be made that Orr simply knew this and merely exploited this weakness. What all of his statements ignored was that a guilty plea did in fact take place.

The plea occurred while Orr held the position of Chief Fire Inspector, yet he does not see this as incriminating. The reason the judge allowed the "uncharged acts" was because the law of California evidence provided him to do so. In California, evidence of "prior bad acts" or bad character traits, can be introduced when it is found to parallel a pattern of behavior. While it certainly can be prejudicial to a jury to hear of his plea bargain, it was impossible to ignore the patterns and devices being found. The pattern of three fires being set per day, the manuscript describing such acts, and the device were all part of Orr's signature behavior.

The plea bargain included the setting of three serial fires in 1987. The first was a Family Bargain Center store, the second was a Craft Mart (hobby store) and a third was at a fabric store. All three fires were set on January 16, 1987. What makes this odd, they resembled the exact pattern of the antagonist, "Aaron Stiles" in Orr's book, "Points of Origin." Additionally, the fires were being set around or near fire investigator conferences. In the case of the 1987 fires, all three were set while Orr attended a conference with fellow investigators. This guilty plea included a further three counts of arson.

The first arson fire was at a Builder's Emporium. There were two other fires were set near the Pacific Coast Highway in Atascadero, California. Orr admitted "I was 40 miles south" which was slightly more than a half hour's drive at a normal rate of travel on any highway. Once again, three serial arson fires took place immediately after the 1989 conference for arson investigators. His fictional account was becoming reality.

There is also the evidence of a partial fingerprint that was found by investigators. We know both from the trial evidence and Orr's statement there was no "John Orr device" found or even kept as evidence which held his fingerprint. However, to ignore the fact that a partial print appeared on yellow lined paper with markings that resembled the exact way the timed device would have been wrapped (see Figure 7) and mirrored the same proportions and measurements as those used during fire seminars, drastically limited the number of suspects.

Although the initial partial print failed to come back as an exact match. The fingerprint was enhanced using ninhydrin, a technique that has been around since 1954. The fact remains that when the print was enhanced, it pointed to one man, John Orr. Orr explained that a fingerprint likely existed, but that it was the probable result of an "innocent touching."

Orr does not admit that the fingerprint evidence was erroneous. It was not planted by someone within his department to make him look guilty. Instead, this print may have be the result of him accidentally touching the yellow lined paper. This is crucial because this paper was found inside the fire. This places the serial arsonist and his fingerprint inside the fire before it ever began.

What is important to understand is that by fully admitting his involvement in these serial fires it would destroy everything he believes, even to this day. His steadfast comments that he was very good at his job and career would be negated. By actually admitting guilt, it would disprove all of his work as a fire investigator and finally substantiate why he was an "early responder" to so many fires (including the fatal Ole's fire) that he solved. The truth would almost render his life meaningless other than being one of the most prolific fire setters in American history.

The danger of acknowledging his guilt would also have a hurricane-like effect on his life behind bars, which is not much after 26 years. The remaining family members who cling to the hope of him being found innocent and providing commissary funds would likely vanish. The few individuals who visit or talk with him could disappear entirely. These thoughts alone are reasons to perpetuate these stories.

If John Orr admitted guilt, it would prove all of the evidence, plea bargained fires and criminal verdicts were indeed correct. For the sparse remaining members of the firefighter brotherhood who still hold Orr in somewhat high regard, it would alienate them beyond imagination.

For a prisoner held in an 8x10 cell, psychologically, this becomes extremely dangerous territory to enter. The walls that his mind has built up as a defense mechanism for three decades would be torn down. An admission of guilt would act like a slow turning vice, ever tightening and never stopping. It therefore becomes far easier to build an elaborate tale than to live with the reality of the truth.

The truth is far likelier that it was indeed John Orr's "homemade device" that set hundreds to thousands of serial arson fires in California. This device was employed by a narcissistic serial arsonist who possessed a high degree of criminal intelligence by using his position of power to look into the investigation. This information allowed him to develop new strategies and vary his targets to avoid detection.

While likely accidental, the fatal fire took four innocent lives. Damages to residential homes, brush, trees, warehouses and other structures exceeded well over $10,000,000 in damages. Businesses, families and homes were lost forever.

A serial arson career spanned a decade or more because it was being investigated by the very person in charge of finding the perpetrator. If there was a single individual who fit the criminal profile and operated in such a manner as to not be detected as the serial arsonist known as the "Pillow Pyro" - it would be John Leonard Orr.

References

Bradford, J. M. (1982). Arson: a clinical study. Canadian Journal of
Psychiatry, 27, 188-193.

Burton's Legal Thesaurus, 4th Ed. (2007) by William C. Burton. Used
with permission of the McGraw-Hill Companies, Inc.

Douglas, J., Burgess, A.W., & Ressler, R. (1992). Crime classification
manual. NY: Lexington Books

Dugan, A. (n.d.) What is the Average Speaking Rate? Retrieved July
11, 2017 from http://sixminutes.dlugan.com/speaking rate/

Federal Emergency Management Agency, United State Fire
Administration, National Fire Data Center, 1997

Lewis, N. O. C., & Yarnell, H. (1951). Pathological fire setting
(pyromania). Nervous and Mental Disease Monograph, 82,
Nicholasville, KY: Coolidge Foundation.

Orr, J., & Wilson, D., (1982) *Working to solve arson's epidemic.*

Western Fire Journal, 19-24.

Index

Made in the USA
Monee, IL
17 June 2022

98169488R00050